This Book
Was Donated By

Christy
Wilson
Summer Reading
Club 2000

2

HOW TO DRAW
ANIMALS

Anita Ganeri and Judy Tatchell

Designed by Steve Page

Illustrated by Claire Wright

Cartoon illustrations by Jon Sayer

Additional illustrations by Rosalind Hewitt

Contents

About this book

Animals may be elegant, cuddly, fierce or exotic. Some are easier to draw than others.

Cartoon pictures usually have a simple outline with exaggerated features.

Big ears

Large beak

Big eyes

If you like animals, you will probably enjoy drawing them. Drawing animals will also help to improve your general drawing skills. This book shows you how to draw and color all kinds of animals in easy step-by-step stages.

Some animals make good cartoons. Their natural characteristics can be exaggerated to make them look funny. Throughout the book there are suggestions for animals which make particularly good cartoons and how to draw and color them.

Professional tips

Throughout the book, there are tips from professional animal illustrators to help you. Here are a couple to start with.

It is easier to draw an animal if you can look at one at the same time but this is not always possible. Animal illustrators often draw from photographs instead of live animals.

Take a sketchbook with you if you visit a farm or a zoo. Sketch details, such as a head or a leg, as well as whole animals.

Picture colored with crayons and watercolors.

Cartoon colored in with felt pens.

Pencil sketch

If you want to draw realistic animals, this book will help you to get the shapes right. You can see how to draw fur, slimy skin, wrinkly hide and so on.

All you need to start drawing is a pencil and paper but there are lots of suggestions throughout the book for further materials to use.

2

Using simple shapes

Animals' bodies look complicated but they are mostly made up of quite simple shapes. In this book you can see how to draw animals using simple shapes and building up the outline around them. Here are some examples.

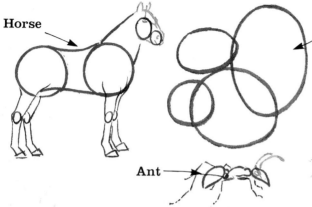

Horse

Squirrel

Ant

The shapes used to draw these animals are made up of rough circles, egg shapes, curves and lines.

Here you can see how the outlines of the animals have been built up around the starting shapes.

A horse's head

Ears are leaf-shaped.

These shapes are like slightly squashed circles.

This is called a construction line. It helps to position the eyes.

Shading makes the face look 3-dimensional.

Try copying the shapes above to draw a horse's head – first the red, then the blue, then the green ones. Draw the lines in faint pencil.

Draw in the outline around the shapes and add more details to the eyes and nose. Sketch in the mane. Color the horse and then add some shading.

You can use watercolor paints or crayons to color the horse. This one was colored in reddish and dark brown crayons over a pale brown watercolor base.

Coloring in

Animals have different types of skin depending on where and how they live. They may have fur to keep them warm or patterned skin for camouflage. Here, you can find out how to use different drawing materials to show fur, skin, hair and so on. The ideas will help you to color in the animals in this book.

Furry coats

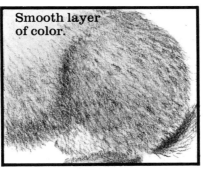

Using watercolor paints, start with a smooth wash of a pale color. Let it dry. Add short strokes of richer and darker color for fur.

If you are using crayons, start with a smooth layer of pale color. Build up the brighter and darker hairs on top, using short strokes.

For black and white pictures, use the side of a soft pencil, such as a 3B*. Use a sharper, harder pencil, such as a 3H*, to add more detail.

Hairy coats

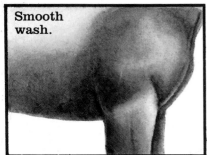

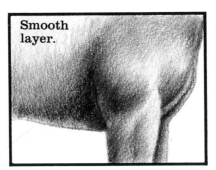

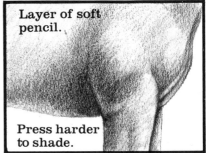

For smooth hair, do a flat wash. Put the main color on top, leaving pale areas for shine. Use a thicker mix of color or a darker shade for shadows.

With crayons, you can keep the texture smooth by using blunt ones. Leave some streaks for shine. Go over shadowed areas again, or use a darker shade.

For black and white pictures, you need a smoother finish than for furry coats. Use a soft pencil, with a harder pencil for the outline.

4   *Pencils range from 9B (very soft) to 9H (very hard).*

Skin

For a brightly colored skin, such as snakeskin, sketch the pattern in light pencil. Then color the pattern in paint or crayon.

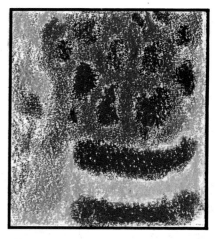

Watercolor wash.

Colors blend at the edges on damp paper.

For a mottled skin, like a frog, use blunt crayons for a soft finish. With paint, add different shades while the paper is still damp.

Wax crayons are useful for drawing bright skins as they give a shiny finish. It is harder to get fine detail with wax crayons, though.

Coloring cartoons

You can color cartoons in bright, flat colors. The detail is in the outline of the cartoon and you don't need to shade them.

Professional tip

Place mask over pencil sketch.

Mask cut out of cardboard

To keep the area around your picture clean while you paint, cut a hole the size of your picture in a piece of thin cardboard. This is called a mask. Place the mask over the picture and color in through the hole. You can test out different shades on the mask.

Cats and dogs

The main feature of a cat's body is its very flexible spine. A dog's spine is straighter. Here are some cats and dogs to practice. Can you see the differences?

A cat

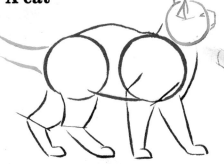

Sketch the markings in pencil before you color them.

Erase unnecessary lines before coloring.

Sketch the shapes above in pencil. Start with the shapes shown in red, then the blue ones, then the green. Don't worry if you cannot get them right at first. Just keep trying.

Smooth off and refine the outline. Add details such as eyes, a nose and whiskers. Begin to color the cat starting with the palest color and building the darker markings on top.

For a marmalade cat use orange, yellow and brown. You could use watercolor for the base and crayon for the fur. Do some streaks of grey to show the fur on the white front and paws.

A dog

The body is leaner than a cat's.

Feathery streaks round the outline make it shaggy.

Putting shadow underneath makes the dog look as if it is standing on the ground.

The starting shapes for a dog are similar to those of a cat but the proportions are slightly different. The nose is longer and the body is less rounded.

The dog's chest is deeper than a cat's. Its underside tapers up towards the back legs. You can see how the tail is really an extension of the backbone.

This is an English Setter. Start with a pale grey, then build up darker streaks and markings on top. Finally, add some white streaks to highlight the long hair.

Comparing cats and dogs

Here you can see how the shapes of cats and dogs differ when they are sitting or lying.

A cat's back is curved when it is sitting. It is curled almost into a circle when it is lying down.

It is easier to draw an animal from the side than from the front.

The dog's back is much straighter than the cat's when it is sitting or lying down.

Cartoon cats and dogs

Cartoon cats and dogs are easier to draw than real ones. Sketch your cartoon in pencil, then go over the outline in black felt pen. Color the cartoon in bright, flat colors.

Puppies and kittens have more rounded bodies than adult cats and dogs.

Horses

Horses are quite difficult to draw. Try the method below. Start with simple shapes using a light pencil until the body is right. Then you can color it in.

Back circle

Front circle

Draw two circles, one slightly bigger than the other. The larger circle is the front of the horse and the smaller one the back. Join them with curved lines to form the body.

Head

Neck

Rounded knee joints.

Extend the larger circle with two tapering lines for the neck. Draw a narrow diamond shape for the front of the head. Draw the tops of the legs with small ovals for the joints.

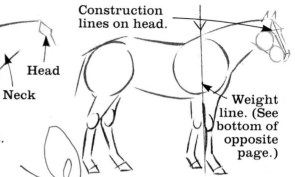

Construction lines on head.

Weight line. (See bottom of opposite page.)

Add the ears, lower legs and the hooves. The green shapes will help you to draw the head. Pencil in construction lines* to position the eyes and nose. You can erase them later.

Long pencil strokes for mane and tail.

Now you can start to add more details to the basic shapes. Do the tail and mane in long pencil strokes. Draw the eye, nostril and mouth. Erase the construction lines.

Shading to show muscles.

See pages 4-5 for more on coloring in.

Show where the horse's muscles are with light shading. Shade underneath the body, too. This makes the animal look more rounded and solid (or 3-dimensional).

Main color

Dark shading

Build up the horse's main color using soft crayon strokes. Leave some white patches for highlights. Use a darker shade of the main color to finish off the shading.

8   *See page 4 for more about construction lines.

Horses in motion

Walking

Head held low.

A front leg is lifted and the opposite back leg is the furthest behind.

Trotting

The head and legs are lifted higher than in a walk. Opposite legs come forward together.

Cantering

The head is stretched out. Opposite legs are flung out in front and behind.

A cartoon horse

Follow the stages below to draw a cartoon horse. Start with block shapes and sticks to get the proportions of the body looking right.

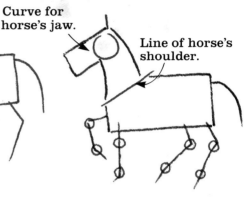

Curve for horse's jaw.

Line of horse's shoulder.

Round off the edges to make the outline more curvy. Exaggerate the ▼ horse's long nose, droopy lips and lumpy body. You can color it in felt pens.

Professional tip

When you are drawing an animal, it can help to draw a construction line which shows where the animal's weight is falling. This helps you to work out how to position the legs and makes the picture look balanced.

9

Farm animals

On these two pages you can see how to draw farm animals and how to turn some of them into cartoons. If you live near a farm, try sketching the live animals. You could practice the ones here first, to get the idea of the shapes.

A cow

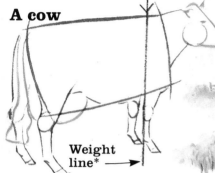

Weight line* ➝

Watercolor paint was used here.

The head is more rounded.

Shallower body.

Long, slender legs.

To draw a cow, pencil in the red, blue and green shapes. It has a heavier body and a shorter neck than a horse. Its neck and spine form a straighter line.

Shade the sandy brown areas. Then do the bluey black patches. When it is dry, go over the darker areas with more bluey black paint.

Use similar basic shapes for a calf but make them smaller. A calf's legs are longer in relation to its body than a cow's. Its body and limbs are more slender.

A cartoon sheep

Egg-shaped head.

Some pale blue shading makes the sheep look more fluffy.

These lambs' legs are furrier than the sheep's.

To draw a cartoon sheep, copy the shapes above. The body is made up of three rounded shapes. Draw sticks to show where the legs go.

Draw a curly outline round the sheep's body to show its woolly coat. Draw in ears and give the face a lazy, sleepy look. Block in the shapes of the legs.

Cartoon lambs are a similar shape to sheep but have longer necks and legs. To make cartoons look more professional, go over the outline with black felt pen.

*The weight line is explained on page 9.

Cartoon ducks and pigs

You can base a cartoon duck shape on triangles and ovals. Build up the feathery outline around them.

Triangles for tail and feet.

Ragged tail feathers.

Ripples show how the duck is moving.

Pigs make good cartoons because it is easy to exaggerate their round, lumbering bodies.

Start with three round shapes.

Triangular ears.

Snout

Fat legs

Cloven hooves

A hen

The hen was colored in a pale brown watercolor wash. The darker patches were then built up on top.

Weight line*

A rooster

Use contrasting colors for the feathers.

Weight line*

This shape is quite tricky to draw.

Start with the red circles. Then draw the hen's back, shown in blue. Then add the other blue lines and the head.

Use long curves for the rooster's body. It has a bigger comb than the hen and more dramatic coloring.

The weight line is explained on page 9.

Countryside creatures

On these pages you can see how to draw a few of the animals that live in the countryside. They are all shy creatures, but some, such as the fox and squirrel, also venture into towns.

Rabbits

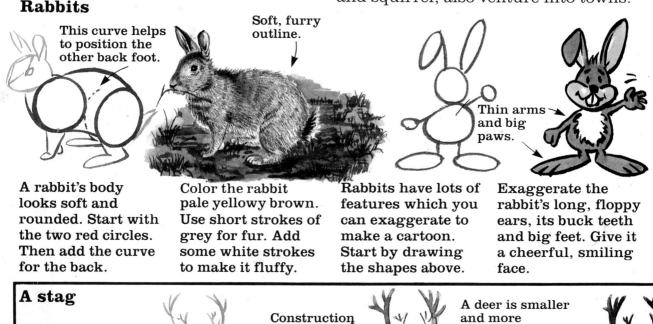

This curve helps to position the other back foot.

Soft, furry outline.

Thin arms and big paws.

A rabbit's body looks soft and rounded. Start with the two red circles. Then add the curve for the back.

Color the rabbit pale yellowy brown. Use short strokes of grey for fur. Add some white strokes to make it fluffy.

Rabbits have lots of features which you can exaggerate to make a cartoon. Start by drawing the shapes above.

Exaggerate the rabbit's long, floppy ears, its buck teeth and big feet. Give it a cheerful, smiling face.

A stag

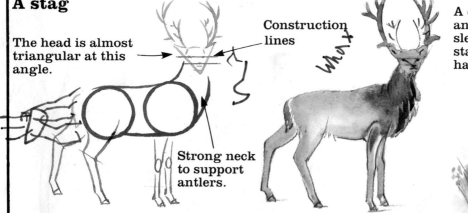

The head is almost triangular at this angle.

Construction lines

Strong neck to support antlers.

A deer is smaller and more slender than this stag. Only stags have antlers.

The basic shapes for a stag are similar to those for a horse, as shown in red above. It holds its head higher, though, and has a strong neck.

Draw the outline round the shapes. Use construction lines to position features on the head. Put down the base color on the body, with some shading.

Add areas of richer reddish brown. Then add dark brown shadows under the body and neck. The antlers are grey with highlights to make them look velvety.

Cartoon hedgehogs

To do a cartoon hedgehog, exaggerate its pointed nose and prickles. Start with an egg shape with a circle at the front, as shown.

A cartoon squirrel

Start with the shapes below for a cartoon squirrel. Then give it round cheeks full of nuts, large front teeth and a bushy tail.

You could add stripes to make it look like a chipmunk.

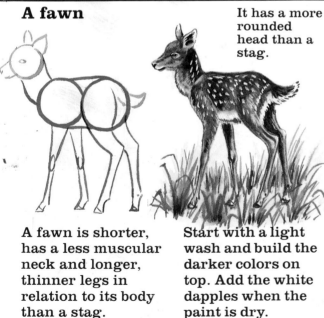

A fawn

It has a more rounded head than a stag.

A fawn is shorter, has a less muscular neck and longer, thinner legs in relation to its body than a stag.

Start with a light wash and build the darker colors on top. Add the white dapples when the paint is dry.

A cartoon fox

This cartoon fox has a wily expression due to its long, pointed nose and hooded eyes. To draw a real fox, you can use the same shapes as for a dog (see pages 6-7).

13

Big cats

All cats have the same basic shape. They have long, streamlined bodies and flexible spines. Look for differences in their head shapes and their markings.

A tiger

The shapes for this tiger are adapted from the cat shape on page 6. Start with the red shapes, then the blue, then the green ones.

Draw the outline of the tiger round the shapes. It has lumpier shoulders and a less rounded head than a domestic cat.

To color it in, start with the lighter color and build up the markings on top. See the box opposite for more about markings.

Heads

Big cats' heads differ more than their bodies. Draw the outlines and construction lines in faint pencil.

The tiger looks like a heavier version of a domestic cat, with a broad face.

Lions have long, heavy faces and chins. Only males have golden manes.

The cheetah has a small, neat head to make its body more streamlined.

The jaguar has round ears. Its mouth and nose form a pear shape.

Cartoon big cats

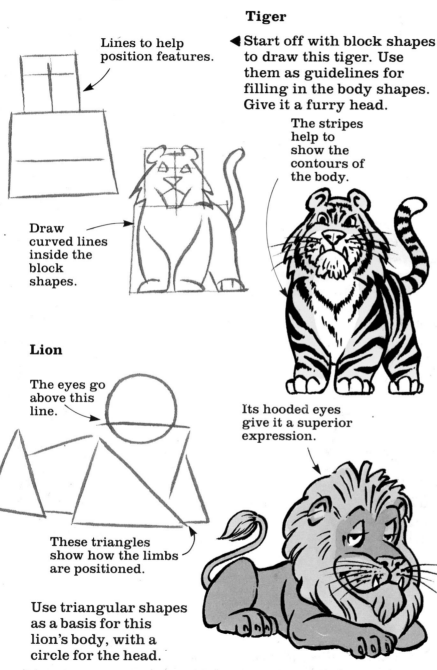

Lines to help position features.

Draw curved lines inside the block shapes.

Tiger

◀ Start off with block shapes to draw this tiger. Use them as guidelines for filling in the body shapes. Give it a furry head.

The stripes help to show the contours of the body.

Its hooded eyes give it a superior expression.

Lion

The eyes go above this line.

These triangles show how the limbs are positioned.

Use triangular shapes as a basis for this lion's body, with a circle for the head.

Markings

Watercolor paint was used for these examples. You could also use soft crayons.

Tiger's stripes added on top of a slightly damp, flat wash.

Hairs in lion's mane added in a richer color on a flat wash.

Cheetah has spots evenly spaced all over body.

Jaguar's markings in rosettes with spots in the middle.

15

Jungle animals

Here you can see how to draw some animals that live in the jungle. If you go to a zoo, try sketching the animals.

Look at how they move and at their expressions. These details will help to make your pictures more realistic.

A gibbon

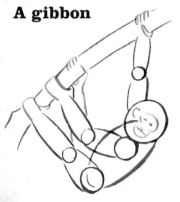

Gibbons have long arms and strong hands and feet to help them grip branches. To draw a gibbon, start with these shapes.

Start to color the gibbon's fur using pale yellowy brown. Make the outline fuzzy using short strokes of a darker color.

Refine the picture by shading and adding more definition to the fur. Add detail to the face, making the features quite sharp.

A gorilla

The gorilla has longer fur than a gibbon.

An orangutan

Gorillas are similar to gibbons, but their bodies and limbs are thicker and heavier. Draw the gorilla's squat shape. Color it in black and white to show the highlights on its fur.

This orangutan is made up of rounded shapes. It has powerful shoulders like the gorilla and a large, broad face. Its head is set low on its shoulders. Color the long, shaggy fur in shades of orangey brown.

Life in the jungle

In this jungle scene you can see how to turn some real animals into cartoons.

Try exaggerating the monkeys' long arms and fingers. Give them human expressions.

For cartoon snakes you can use vivid, contrasting colors for their markings.

Draw a menacing cartoon crocodile hiding in the water. Exaggerate its bulbous eyes and sharp teeth.

A crocodile

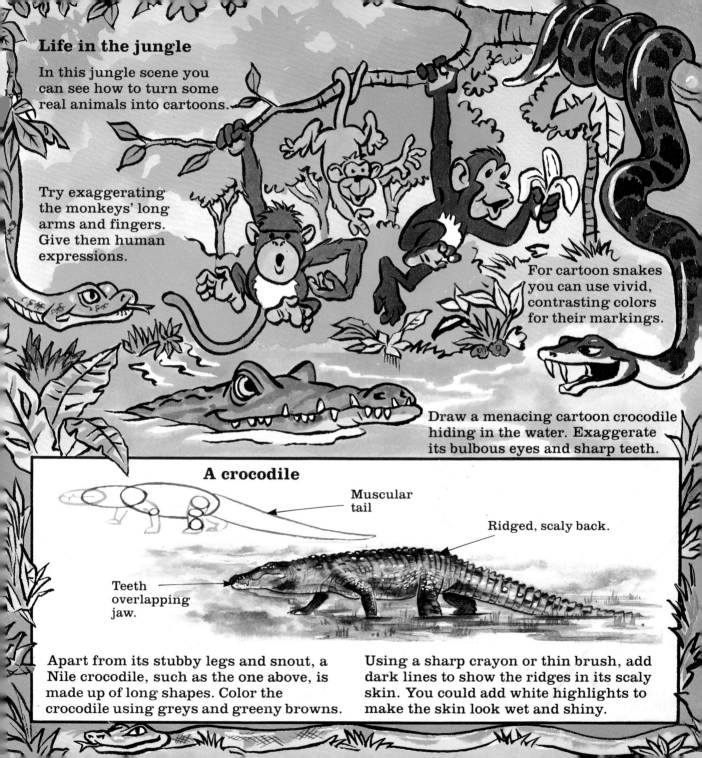

Muscular tail

Ridged, scaly back.

Teeth overlapping jaw.

Apart from its stubby legs and snout, a Nile crocodile, such as the one above, is made up of long shapes. Color the crocodile using greys and greeny browns.

Using a sharp crayon or thin brush, add dark lines to show the ridges in its scaly skin. You could add white highlights to make the skin look wet and shiny.

Desert animals

Many animals that live in the desert have special features which help them to survive in hot, dry conditions.

Snakes and lizards

Some reptiles' bright skins warn off predators. Others are colored to blend in with their surroundings. Try to work out the basic shapes for yourself.

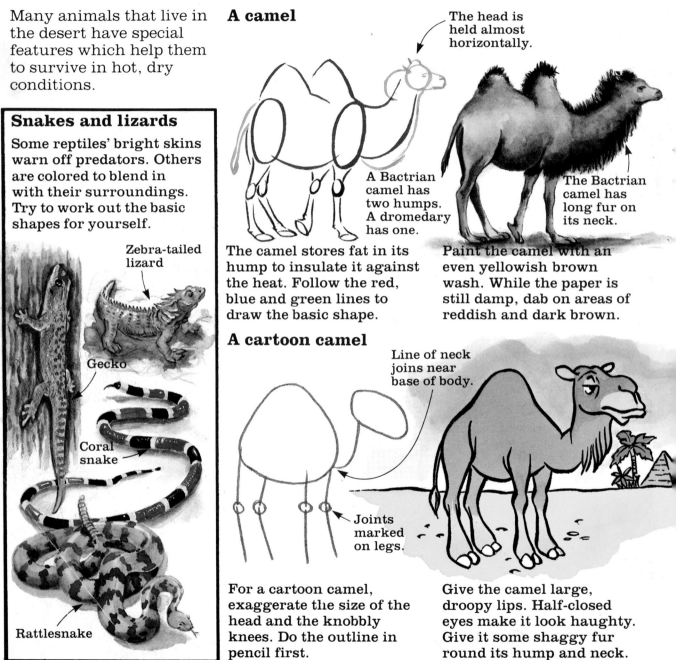

Zebra-tailed lizard

Gecko

Coral snake

Rattlesnake

A camel

The head is held almost horizontally.

A Bactrian camel has two humps. A dromedary has one.

The Bactrian camel has long fur on its neck.

The camel stores fat in its hump to insulate it against the heat. Follow the red, blue and green lines to draw the basic shape.

Paint the camel with an even yellowish brown wash. While the paper is still damp, dab on areas of reddish and dark brown.

A cartoon camel

Line of neck joins near base of body.

Joints marked on legs.

For a cartoon camel, exaggerate the size of the head and the knobbly knees. Do the outline in pencil first.

Give the camel large, droopy lips. Half-closed eyes make it look haughty. Give it some shaggy fur round its hump and neck.

18

Small animals

Small, furry animals usually have rounded bodies. You can adapt the mouse shape on the right to draw hamsters and guinea pigs.

A mouse

◀ To color the mouse, paint a sandy brown wash over it. Leave it to dry and then use a darker brown pencil to draw short strokes for the fur.

Beady black eyes.

A guinea pig

▲
A guinea pig is made up of chunkier shapes than the mouse. This one is a long-haired variety. Sketch faint lines showing how the hair should lie before you paint it.

A hamster

A hamster is larger and rounder than a mouse. Paint it with a watery light brown. When it is dry, paint strokes of fur in a stronger mix of the same color. Then do the darker areas on top.
▼

A cartoon mouse

A mouse makes a good cartoon because you can exaggerate its big ears and nose and its long tail. See if you can work out the basic shapes for this mouse yourself.

More wild animals

Here are some real and cartoon pictures of several wild animals. They all have different shapes and so will give you good drawing practice.

A kangaroo

Use very watery white paint for the highlights.

A cartoon kangaroo

The kangaroo's weight is centered over its back legs. It uses its heavy tail for balance.

After you have painted the body reddish brown, add white highlights and dark shadows.

Movement lines

To draw a cartoon kangaroo, you can exaggerate its huge feet, short arms and big nose. Draw movement lines to show that it is bounding along. This kangaroo has a baby in its pouch enjoying the ride.

A cartoon aardvark

An aardvark's strange but simple shape makes it a good cartoon. This one has a long snout and big ears.

A zebra

A zebra has a similar shape to the horse on page 8. Its body is slightly shorter, though, and it has a very short mane.

All zebras are stripy but the patterns can differ. Use a pencil to sketch in the markings on your zebra's coat.

Giraffes

A giraffe has plenty ▶ of features which you can exaggerate for a cartoon. Its body is a funny shape with a long neck, small head and stumpy horns.

To draw a real giraffe, start with the rough triangular shape shown in red. Then add the shapes for the legs and head. ▼

See the box below for a hint on how to color in the giraffe's markings.

Color the zebra in using paints or crayons. A zebra's stripes provide it with camouflage behind long stalks of grass so that from a distance it is hidden from hunting lions.

Professional tip

When using watercolor paints for an animal's markings, try wetting the paper first with clean water. Paint the color on while it is still damp. The different areas of color will merge together at the edges, giving a softer impression.

21

Big animals

You can practice drawing tough, wrinkled hides on the elephant and hippo on these pages.

Many big animals also make good cartoons because of their lumbering, heavy shapes.

An elephant

This African elephant has larger ears than an Indian elephant.

Start with the shapes above – first the red shapes, then the blue ones and then the green ones.

Paint the elephant with a grey watercolor wash. Keeping the paper damp, dab on some sandy brown patches and darker grey shadows. When it is dry, add the wrinkles. Alternatively you could use crayons. Keep the base colors smooth and use a sharp crayon for the wrinkles.

A cartoon rhino

Horns Ears

The steps above will help you to draw a cartoon rhino. For the body, start with four overlapping ovals (egg shapes).

Add sticks to show where the legs go. Then mark in the positions of the horns and ears, as shown in pencil above.

You can then draw in the eyes, mouth, legs and tail. Go over the outline in black felt pen and then color the rhino in.

22

A cartoon elephant

A cartoon elephant looks like a simplified version of a real one. You could make your elephant look almost human by drawing it reading a newspaper or dancing, like the one above.

A cartoon whale

Start with the shape shown in red to draw a cartoon whale. Draw the whale half-submerged in the sea, squirting water out of its blow-hole. Draw its tail fins jutting out from below the surface.

A hippopotamus

Add the wrinkles and color the features when the rest of the colors are dry.

The hippo is a similar shape to the elephant, but it has a squatter body and stubbier legs. It holds its head down low.

Paint washes of grey and pinky brown. Blend the edges by dipping a brush in water and "feathering" the colors together.

A cartoon hippo

Try drawing a cartoon based on the shapes for the real hippo. Emphasize its jaw and make its legs shorter and fatter.

23

Bears

Here you can see how to draw three famous types of bear. Look at pages 4-5 for some hints on coloring in fur.

A brown bear

Some brown bears stand up to 8ft tall on their hind legs. They are a similar shape to polar bears. This bear was colored with light brown, reddish brown and dark brown crayon.

A polar bear

The polar bear is one of the strongest animals in the world. Its rounded body is covered in thick fur.

Shade the body with pale yellow and bluey grey to make it stand out on white paper.

A cartoon panda

You can use a panda's vivid markings to make a striking cartoon. Pandas eat bamboo, so you could draw it surrounded by shoots.

Cuddly animals

Small, furry animals look cuddly because of their size and softness. These ones are made up of rounded shapes.

Koala bears

This koala bear, with its baby on its back, is climbing a eucalyptus tree. Draw the shapes for the mother first and then position the baby.

Bluey black and brown watercolors were used here for a soft effect.

Keep the paper damp so the colors blend.

A baby loris

White dots in the eyes make them look shiny.

A baby loris has big brown eyes and a furry coat. Draw a faint outline so that when you color it in there are no hard edges. Use long strokes of a darker color to make it look fluffy.

A seal cub

Draw the seal's body and head shape first, and then position the flippers. Seal cubs have soft, furry white coats. They lose the fur as they get older.

Chicks

Chicks have big feet compared to their bodies. Color them rich yellow, then use orangey brown to shade them and to define the fluffy feathers.

25

Creepy crawlies

Many people find creepy crawlies repulsive. Some have beautiful details on their bodies, though, such as fine veins on their wings, or colored markings.

Spiders

This is a garden spider.

A spider's body is made up of ovals with lines for the legs, as shown by the colored shapes over to the right.

This spider was painted in watercolors. Start with a pale wash and build up the darker shades on top. Leave a white cross on its back.

You could draw a huge tarantula hanging from its web. Exaggerate its hairy legs, bulging eyes and round body.

An ant

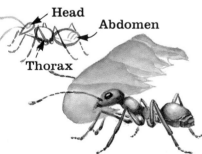

Head

Abdomen

Thorax

All insects' bodies are divided into three parts, called the head, thorax and abdomen. Draw the rough shapes for an ant and color them as shown.

A wasp

All insects have six legs which join on to the thorax.

Tiny veins in wings.

A wasp's body is a similar shape to an ant's but its head and abdomen are more curved. It has delicate wings. Its vivid colors warn off enemies.

Bees

Bees have fatter, rounder bodies and smaller wings than wasps. They are covered in tiny hairs. Try a cartoon bee as well as a real one.

A grasshopper

Male grasshoppers "sing" by rubbing their hind legs together.

There are about one million types of insect in the world.

A grasshopper's back legs are large and strong to help it jump a long way. It has a straighter back than ants, wasps or bees.

To color it in, start with a pale shade of green. Build up the deeper shades on top. Then add dark lines to show its hard covering.

Caterpillars

A snail

Draw in the spiral of the snail's shell.

The white streaks on the snail's shell make it look hard and shiny. Draw a glistening trail of slime behind the snail.

A cockroach

A cockroach has a hard, shiny black or brown covering, so make it shiny. Draw fine hairs on its legs and give it long antennae.

Caterpillars are made up of lots of segments which get narrower towards the head. This one has bright streaks to warn off predators.

Long, hairy caterpillars make good cartoons.

27

Animals that swim

Here you can see how to draw some animals which live in or near water. Fish have simple shapes but you can color them brightly. You can also try more complicated creatures such as penguins, seahorses and turtles.

A shark

To draw this cartoon shark, start with the outline above. Sharks have sleek, streamlined bodies to help them move quickly through the water. Draw the fin jutting out above the water.

Gills

Position the other fins and the gills. Draw a curve in the tail. The top part is longer and narrower than the bottom part. The shark's sharp, triangular teeth slope backwards.

More cartoon fish

These tropical fish show variations on the fish shape and some ideas for color. Give them exotic fins and tails.

An octopus

Try copying this giant octopus resting on the sea bed. It has an egg-shaped head and eight legs covered in suckers.

Penguins

To draw realistic penguins, use the shapes shown on the right. Their bodies are smooth and streamlined. Their small flippers make them look comical. To draw the icy water, do blue watercolor streaks. Then dip your brush in water and "feather" the color out.

Add eyes when paint is dry.

Pale shading on bodies.

A turtle

Watercolor on body.

Delicate crayoning on head and fins.

A turtle's shape is made up of an oval for the body and leaf shapes for the flippers and head. The shell looks like armor-plating.

A seahorse

A seahorse has an S-shaped body and very fine fins. Highlight the ridges on its body with white paint.

Frogs

Compare the real frog above and the cartoon. The bulging eyes and wide mouth are made more prominent.

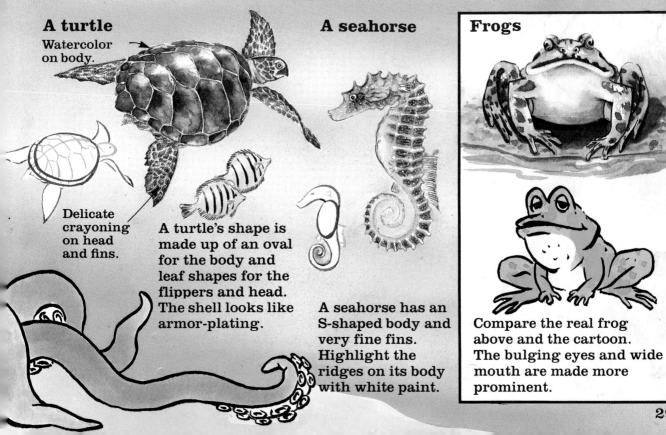

Animals that fly

All the animals on these two pages can fly but their body and wing shapes differ widely. Some of them have beautiful markings which are fun to color in.

Birds

Head, body and tail form a straight line.

These are the basic shapes for a tern. Look at other birds to see how their shapes differ.

The tern is white except for its head, beak and feet. Shade its body with a pale bluey grey.

You can adapt the shapes to do birds in other positions. Remember that the wings grow out from the bird's spine. They always bend in the same place and curve slightly backwards.

Feathers

Feather shapes in brown watercolor.

Details added in crayon.

Practice drawing a bird's wing in close up. Use short strokes of colored crayon or paint to show the detail on the feathers.

An owl

Heart shapes for the body and head.

This owl was colored with dabs of reddish and dark brown paint on damp paper. Paler strokes show its downy breast.

A flamingo

The flamingo's beak, neck and body form a rough S-shape. Color it in shades of pink, using pale blue for the shadows.

A cartoon toucan

Draw rough shapes in pencil for the beak and body until the proportions look right. Then refine the outline.

You could color it in any shades you like.

Butterflies

Pastels give a powdery look.

To draw butterflies in different positions, copy the red shape on paper and cut it out. Fold it to the position you want, then look at it as you draw. These were colored in artist's pastels.

A peacock

Use a very thin brush for the feathers.

Detail of "eye".

Start the peacock by drawing a large oval on its side, in light pencil. Then draw a body in the middle and color the feathers.

Cartoon bats

For this scene, copy or trace these bat silhouettes. Color them in black wax crayon, then go over them in a dark blue watercolor wash.

Index

First published in 1987 by Usborne Publishing Ltd,
Usborne House, 83-85 Saffron Hill, London EC1N 8RT, England.

Copyright © Usborne Publishing Ltd. 1987

The name Usborne and the device ⬮ are Trade Marks of
Usborne Publishing Ltd.

Printed in Belgium AE